A for a Day

WENDY DOUTHWAITE

Illustrated by David Browne

PACIFIC
LEARNING

© 2001 Pacific Learning
© 1999 Written by **Wendy Douthwaite**
Illustrated by **David Browne**
US Edit by **Rebecca Weber McEwen**

All rights reserved. No part of this publication may
be reproduced or transmitted in any form or by
any means, electronic or mechanical, including
photocopying, recording, taping, or any information
storage and retrieval system, without permission in
writing from the publisher.

This Americanized Edition of *A Dog for a Day*,
originally published in English in 1999, is published
by arrangement with Oxford University Press.

05 04 03 02 01
10 9 8 7 6 5 4 3 2 1

Published by
Pacific Learning
P.O. Box 2723
Huntington Beach, CA 92647-0723
www.pacificlearning.com

ISBN: 1-59055-062-5
PL-7507

Contents

CHAPTER 1

The Rescue

It was Saturday, and Mom wasn't going to work. Even though she was trying to be cheerful, Mark could see the worry in her eyes. He shifted uncomfortably on his stool. If only he could do something.

"I think I'll go see Dan," Mark said, sliding down from the stool, and slipping quietly out the back door.

It was a relief to be outside. He felt as though he needed to be quiet – almost as though Dad were very ill.

Dad had lost his job six months ago. After twenty-three years at Higgins Incorporated, his job had been taken over by a machine, and suddenly Dad was at home all the time.

At first, it had been fun, but lately all the joy had gone out of Dad. He just paced up and down the living room like a caged animal, always searching the Help Wanted ads in the local newspaper.

Mark cheered up a little as he approached Dan's house. Dan was twelve, the same age as Mark. He was fun, and he was Mark's best friend.

When he knocked on the door, Dan's mother opened it. She looked surprised. "My goodness, Mark, I thought you had gone too," she said.

For a moment, Mark was puzzled.
Then he remembered. Of course – she
meant the school field trip. He had
completely forgotten. He hadn't gone
because Mom and Dad couldn't afford
to pay for it. Mark turned away, feeling
more miserable than ever.

"Come over tomorrow, Mark, okay?"
Dan's mother called after him anxiously,
for she had seen the look on his face.
Mark nodded and waved.

Pushing his hands into his pockets, Mark scuffed along the pavement, not knowing where to go next. He kicked at an empty can, which clattered noisily along the gutter.

Almost without realizing it, Mark found his feet turning toward the town garbage dump. It was a bleak place.

Pieces of paper blew around, and the big dumpsters were gathered in one corner, like a herd of angry animals.

The truck parking lot next to the dump was where Mark and Dan raced their bikes. It was their favorite place, but today, the lot was deserted.

That was when Mark saw the dog. It was tied to the wire fence. Mark stared. Was it really a dog? Yes, of course it was. It was such a drab color – the color of the ground – and it didn't move. It could almost have been an old piece of material.

Mark took a few steps toward the dog. It was lying down, with its nose resting on its paws. Mark hesitated. Then he walked toward it again.

At last, the dog wearily raised his head. He looked at Mark, dully, from sad brown eyes.

"Hello," Mark said gently, squatting down beside the dog.

He remembered what his mother had often said. "Don't touch strange dogs, Mark – they're not all friendly like old Basil." Basil was Grandma's dog – a big shaggy creature with a wagging tail and a wide grin.

The little dog put his head down again, watching Mark. His eyes didn't dance like Basil's did. They looked tired and wary.

"What are you doing here?" Mark asked. "I won't hurt you, you know."

Then came a screeching of brakes, and the crunch of gravel against rubber tires. The little dog turned frightened eyes in the direction of the sound.

"Look! It's still there!"

Mark recognized the voice. Turning, he saw Wayne Waring from the grade above him at school. Wayne was a bully and Mark was afraid of him.

The older boy flung his bike down on the ground and swaggered over to where Mark stood beside the little dog.

"That thing was there yesterday,"
Wayne told Mark, "and the day before."

Mark was shocked. "What – tied up?"
he asked, adding, "Why didn't you tell
somebody?"

The other boy sneered at Mark. "I
have better things to do," he said. With
a scowl he added, "I hate dogs."

He kicked the ground with his shoe,
sending a shower of dirt and gravel
against the dog's face.

The little dog tried to blink the dirt out of his eyes as he shrank back against the fence.

Wayne laughed.

Anger flared up inside Mark. "Leave him alone!" he shouted, pushing at the other boy.

At once, he was hurled to the ground.

"Don't you ever touch me again, runt," Wayne snarled.

Mark felt a pain in his left leg where he had landed on a stone. Wayne kicked some more dirt at the dog's face and lifted his foot as if to kick him.

Getting his breath back, Mark scrambled up and hurled himself at the older boy. He grabbed him around the legs and Wayne fell to the ground. He was heavy, and the fall winded him.

Mark sat on him and pushed his face into the ground, rage masking his fear.

Wayne was not used to anyone standing up to him. He tried to get up, but Mark angrily kept mashing his face back into the dirt.

"You… leave… that dog… alone… you monster!" Mark panted.

He was amazed to see a tear coming from the corner of one of Wayne's eyes, followed by another, and then another.

"Get off. Leave me alone," the bigger boy whimpered.

Mark was still angry. "Then you better leave him alone," he hissed into Wayne's dirty, tear-smeared face.

"Okay. I will."

Stepping aside to let Wayne scramble to his feet, Mark watched him warily, but he didn't need to worry.

The older boy sullenly turned away and picked up his bike. He pedaled off in the direction of the road.

Mark brushed himself off and rubbed his sore leg. Then he turned back toward the little dog. It cowered against the fence, trembling with fear. As he thought of what Wayne had told him, Mark's heart ached for the little creature.

"How could someone have just left you here?" Mark said softly. He noticed again how thin the little dog was.

Carefully, he stretched out a hand and stroked the dog's head.

The dog trembled and looked up at Mark with frightened eyes. Mark went on stroking the dog's head, tickling him gently behind the ears. The little dog just stayed where he was, huddled up against the rusty fence.

Mark's fingers felt the thick, rough string that was around the dog's neck. It was tied to a piece of wire, which was twisted around the fence. There were marks on the wire where the little dog had tried to chew himself free.

"Poor little thing, you're a prisoner, aren't you?" Mark began untwisting the wire from the fence.

"Come on," he gently urged the dog. He had the end of the wire in his hand. "You can come with me now."

The dog stood up and took a few steps forward, but his legs were unsteady.

Forgetting all his mother's words of warning, Mark gathered the animal into his arms.

The dog felt light and lay quietly in Mark's arms, as the boy carried him out of the parking lot.

He made his way home. He knew Mom would help him…

"Oh, Mark, I'm sorry, not today. You'll have to take it to an animal shelter or something."

Mom's eyes were dark with worry. Mark could see she was thinking about other things. Behind her was Dad, his head slumped over the kitchen table.

Mom put an arm on Mark's shoulder. "I can't think about anything else right now," she explained. "Your dad is so fed up – I don't know what to do. Take it down to the police station, Mark – that's where people report lost dogs."

"But, Mom, he's not lost. Someone left him at the dump – on purpose. He's been there for three days!"

Mark was sure his mother would
listen now, but she was already turning
back toward the kitchen.

"Mark, we can't deal with this right
now," she said. "Just take the dog away."

CHAPTER 2

Bert's Idea

The sidewalk to the police station was steep, and Mark was getting tired from carrying the dog.

Inside the police station, a policeman was sitting at a desk. There was a small bell, with a sign next to it that said, "Please ring for assistance."

Balancing the dog in his arms, Mark tapped the bell. At once, the policeman looked up.

"What can I do for you, young man?" he asked, and Mark explained.

"I see…" The policeman wrote the details on a form, including Mark's name and address. He looked down at the little brown dog in Mark's arms. Mark noticed the man had kind eyes.

"Well, we haven't had any lost dogs reported this week," he said. He looked at the dog.

"It seems as though someone didn't want you. You look like a nice little fellow." He turned to Mark.

"I'm afraid we get a lot of this. People get a dog, and then they decide they can't keep it for some reason, or they get tired of it."

With his free hand, Mark stroked the dog's shabby fur. "But why tie him up like that and… just leave him there to die?" he asked bitterly.

The policeman scratched his head slowly before replying. "People sometimes don't think. That's the trouble, son," he said. "They don't always mean to be cruel."

The policeman looked hard at the dog in Mark's arms. "Now, what in the world are we going to do with you? We're really busy right now, and I don't know where to put him. Never mind," he added, picking up the telephone. "I'll find somewhere. You just wait there for a moment, Mark."

Mark sat down thankfully. The little dog leaned against him, almost as though he had begun to trust him. The thin little body felt warm against his chest.

That was when Mark saw an old man shuffling past the police station. It was Mr. Shubert! The sight of him gave Mark a sudden idea.

Maybe Mr. Shubert would let Mark keep the dog in his shed.

When Mark explained his idea, the policeman was pleased. "I haven't been able to find a place for the dog yet," he told Mark.

He looked out at Mr. Shubert. "Yes, he loves animals, doesn't he?

"I remember how he missed his little dog after it was run over by a car. He kept coming in to ask us if we'd found it yet! Poor old guy. Maybe he'll give the dog a home for now. I'll ask the animal control officer to call…"

Mark hurried after Mr. Shubert. The little brown dog leaned his head against Mark's neck. Mark felt a warm glow of happiness.

Maybe he would be able to keep this little dog after all. Maybe Mom would change her mind in a day or so…

Then Mark began to worry. Maybe Mr. Shubert would say no. Hopefully he wouldn't, but he only had his pension to live on – and dogs cost money.

Mark frowned and his steps slowed as this new worry filled his mind. The little dog in his arms felt so thin – he must have some food, and soon. Mark looked around him.

He was right by the Rose and Crown, the restaurant where Mom and Dad used to go to before Dad lost his job.

Mark remembered going there on Saturdays with Mom and Dad.

When he was little, Mark had played in the patio area at the back, and Dad had ordered the family sodas and hamburgers with fries...

Mark stopped. Another idea had entered his mind.

There was food at this restaurant. Maybe there would be food in the alley at the back – scraps that nobody wanted. It was worth a look!

Mark wandered around to the fence in the back of the restaurant. No one was around. He came to the opening that led to the patio, and then he stopped. Of course, no one would be in the patio in February – how stupid of him.

Then he saw the garbage cans. There were six of them, in a neat row outside the back door of the Rose and Crown.

Mark hesitated. He didn't think it would hurt to peek inside them. The dog in his arms needed food.

His mind made up, he stepped up to the first can and lifted the lid. A smell of rotting food wafted up but Mark was determined. He peered inside.

A sudden noise of a door opening made Mark jump, and he dropped the lid with a clatter. Then he heard a man's voice.

"Hey there – what are you doing?"

Mark wanted to run, but he didn't. He stayed where he was. All at once, he knew the voice. It was Bert Rogers, his dad's old friend who managed the place.

"Aren't you Pete Sakic's youngest? Mark, isn't it?" the man said. Mark nodded. "What do you have there?" He looked closely at the little brown dog.

"I – I found him," Mark began.

Suddenly, he felt that Bert Rogers could be someone who'd understand, and he told him the whole story.

He told him about the parking area, about the fight, about Dad being out of work and how worried Mom was, and how she had said that he couldn't keep the little dog at home.

"Well," Bert Rogers said when Mark paused for breath, "you seem to have had a pretty busy morning, Mark."

Mark nodded, holding tightly to his dog. He had a feeling, somehow, that this man would help him.

"Now first things first," Bert said. "I think we ought to find little Scruffy something to eat – and to drink." He studied the dog for a moment. "In fact," he went on, "I think we ought to give him a drink first, and maybe only a little food to begin with."

Mark looked puzzled, so Bert explained. "We don't know how long he's been without food and water. Water is very important, you know."

The man set off toward the restaurant door. "Now just follow me, and I'll see what I can find."

Bert took Mark into a big kitchen.

"Animals aren't normally allowed in here," he explained, "but we'll break the rules just this once. Now you sit there a moment, Mark."

Mark sat on a chair in the corner of the room while the man fetched an old tin pan and filled it with water.

Mark had never seen a dog drink so quickly.

"Steady now, little Scruff," Bert said, moving the dish away. "I think that's enough for right now."

Turning to Mark he said, "We won't give him any food just yet. I'll give you some to take with you. Give him a little bit at first – about a handful – and then some more later on, and some more water, of course. After all that time without food or water, it will make him sick if he has too much all at once."

Mark was listening carefully.

"I didn't know that," he admitted.

"It's a good thing you came around here then, isn't it," Bert laughed. He stroked the brown dog's head.

The door into the restaurant opened suddenly, letting in the comfortable noise of laughter and clinking silverware.

A plump woman came into the kitchen, carrying a tray loaded with empty plates. She was in a hurry.

"Oh, Bert, come on," she panted, "where have you been? I can't manage on my own..."

Then she saw Mark and his dog. "I might have guessed," she chuckled, coming over to her husband.

"Bert Rogers – you've found another stray dog, haven't you? He's a softy for anything lost or hurt," she explained to Mark. "He's always carting them home to bring back to health and happiness."

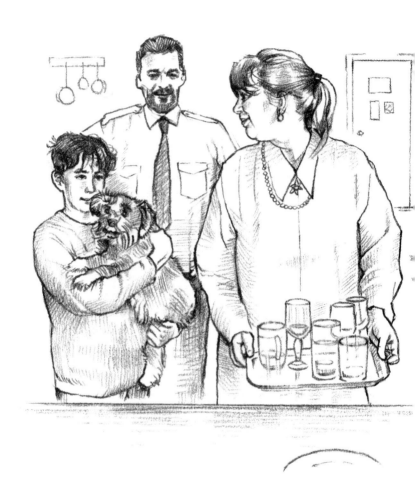

She smiled warmly at Mark. "You're
not lost too, are you?" she asked.

Mark grinned back and shook his head. He liked this woman – she was so warm and friendly.

"Poor little thing," Bert's wife then said, patting the brown dog. "You look very thin and sad. I guess you've had a pretty rotten time."

"I'll tell you what," Bert said. "I'll go and finish my work – it's nearly the end of the lunch rush – and I'll come back. We'll give him a small meal then, Mark. But in the meantime, you tell Mary all about poor little Scruffy here, and when I get back, I'll tell you both about my fantastic idea!"

CHAPTER 3

Mr. Shubert

Mark had a lot to carry as he hurried along the road toward Mr. Shubert's house, but his heart was light.

Bert and Mary Rogers had packed a basket of food, which hung over Mark's arm, and he still carried the little brown dog, who was starting to look a whole lot happier.

Mark had begun to think of him now as Scruffy, even though it wasn't much of a name.

All morning he'd been trying to think of something better, but somehow nothing was right. Then, as Bert and Mary Rogers talked to the dog, the name seemed to fit.

"Okay, Scruffy," Bert had said, "eat up."

The little brown dog gobbled up the scraps, licking the dish right across the kitchen floor.

Mary laughed and said, "I think Scruffy's going to eat the dish too!"

The dog looked up at them with brighter eyes. His thin face, with those funny tufts of hair over his eyes, gave him a puzzled look.

When Mark called, "Scruffy!" the dog turned toward him. "I think he likes his name," Mark said. So, Scruffy it was.

Now they were nearing Mr. Shubert's place. Everyone knew Mr. Shubert, but no one knew quite how old he was. Mom thought he was close to ninety.

Before Dad had lost his job, Mom had often sent Mark over to check on Mr. Shubert and take him some food.

The old man didn't care if Mark brought food or not – he just enjoyed the company. He'd always pushed aside piles of newspapers on the couch and told Mark to "sit down awhile, my boy, and talk to me for a spell!"

Mark knocked on the back door. "Mr. Shubert, it's Mark. Can I come in?" he shouted.

"Yes, come in, my boy. It's a real and rare pleasure to see you!"

Mark made his way through the tiny kitchen. On the stove, a pot of soup was boiling, filling the room with steam.

With his spare hand, Mark reached out and turned off the stove. Poor old Mr. Shubert! One of these days, people said, he would have to go into a retirement home. For the time being, volunteers came twice a week to clean up his house, and the Meals-on-Wheels ladies arrived every weekday with food for him.

"It's good to see you!" Mr. Shubert's faded blue eyes twinkled at Mark. "What's that you've got?" He peered at Scruffy. "Oh, these old eyes of mine! Is that a spare mop or a spare dog?"

Mark sat down beside his old friend and told him Scruffy's story. Mr. Shubert looked grim, even while he stroked Scruffy's neck.

"Well I never," he said, shaking his head, when Mark had finished his tale. "Imagine that! The poor little dog – I never heard such a sad tale."

Almost an hour later, as he hurried home, Mark realized with sudden surprise how hungry he was. It was nearly dinnertime, and his last meal had been breakfast – which felt like days ago!

He broke into a trot and hurried down the sidewalk to the back door. Then he remembered Dad and his pace slowed.

He thought of Mom's worried face and Dad with his head in his hands. Had Bert done what he had promised?

Mom had her back to him. She was taking something out of the oven.

"Hey, is that a chocolate cake?" Mark exclaimed, as his mother turned around, holding the cake pan.

At once, Mark could see that Bert must have dropped by to talk to them, just as he'd promised.

Mom's face glowed with happiness. All the worry and strain were gone.

"Yes, my dear, it is," she replied. "Your favorite! Just give me ten minutes, and I'll get it frosted and ready." She put down the pan and gave Mark a hug.

"You know all about it, don't you? It's so wonderful – I can hardly believe it. Your dad's old friend, Bert Rogers, came to see us."

Mom's face was radiant as she continued. "He told us all about his bartender leaving suddenly yesterday, without giving any notice.

"It's a regular job, Mark – full time and permanent. Dad's a different person already!" Mom could hardly stop smiling.

Dad came in and Mark could see that Mom was right. His eyes were lit with the old fun and interest. He also gave Mark a hug.

"You're amazing, Mark! How did you manage it? After all these months of looking and reading newspapers, and then *you* come up with a job for me, just like that!"

Dad began to set the table for dinner as he talked. "It'll be really nice to have a change. The restaurant's just down the road. There will be no more traveling, and I don't mind the odd hours."

He stopped and laid a hand on Mark's shoulder. "By the way, I'm sorry," he said seriously. "If I'd known I was going to get a job, you could have gone on your school field trip."

"It's okay, Dad," Mark said quickly. "I wouldn't have found Scruffy if I'd gone."

"Is that the dog you found?" Mom asked, and Mark nodded.

Turning to Mark's dad, she said, "What do you think, Pete? Can he keep his little dog?"

"Of course he can," Dad agreed. "Where is he, Mark?"

That night, as Mark lay in bed, he couldn't stop thinking about Scruffy.

The little dog belonged to him now. Tomorrow he would go and bring him back home.

He imagined himself with Scruffy always at his heels. Mark and Scruffy, always together.

His mind leaped ahead to the summer. He and Dan would have all sorts of great adventures with Scruffy.

They would go out to the country, taking backpacks filled with their lunch. They would stay all day, and Scruffy would run in the fields and chase birds he would never catch...

At last, worn out from his busy day, Mark fell asleep. In all his dreams there was a small, brown face, with pale brown tufts of hair sticking out, above bright brown eyes.

CHAPTER 4

Scruffy's New Home

The next morning, as soon as Mark's mind was awake enough to remember Scruffy, he pulled on his clothes and hurried downstairs.

"Wow! You're up early," Mom said.

"I'm going to Mr. Shubert's to get Scruffy," Mark reminded her.

Mom looked at the clock. "Well, don't go there this early," she warned. "You don't want to wake him."

Mark poured cereal into a bowl. "I'll go see Dan first," he said.

Outside, it was raining. Mark pulled his hood over his head and set off down the road toward Dan's house.

Dan's mother opened the door. "Come on in, Mark," she said, smiling warmly. "What a day! Dan's not up yet. He was home pretty late last night. You're an early bird, aren't you?"

Mark bounded up the stairs to Dan's bedroom. "Wake up, lazybones," he shouted, shaking the mound of blankets that was Dan.

Dan sat up in bed, looking at Mark sleepily. "It's still night," he mumbled.

"No it isn't, silly, it's just raining!"

"Oh, come on – this is pretty early for a Sunday, isn't it?" Dan yawned.

"I know, but I have something special to do this morning, and you are coming with me!"

Excitement bubbled inside Mark, as he and Dan splashed through the rain toward Mr. Shubert's house.

He could hardly keep from running. He jumped from side to side of the puddles, and up and down from the curb to the gutter.

Dan was still sleepy. "What's the big rush for?" he complained.

Mark started to tell him about Scruffy. He told his friend about his fight with Wayne Waring.

"Wow!" Dan opened his brown eyes wide with admiration. "He'll sic his gang of friends on you," he warned.

"No he won't," Mark replied. "He knows I'll tell them that he cried. Anyway," he added happily, "I don't care. I've got Scruffy."

They reached Mr. Shubert's house, and Mark pushed open the gate. He began to run as he passed the back door. He made his way toward the shed in the backyard, followed by Dan.

The door was not quite shut. With worry gnawing at his stomach, Mark pushed it open.

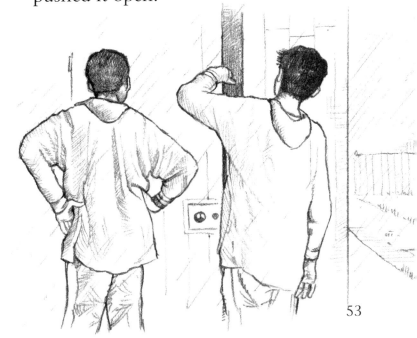

Scruffy was gone! The blanket was there, which Mr. Shubert had found for Scruffy to sleep on. It was dented where the little dog had been lying, and there were even a few brown hairs on it. But Scruffy wasn't there.

Mark's eyes stung with hot tears, and he pushed them back fiercely with his knuckles.

"I don't see any dog," Dan said, as Mark turned and pushed past him.

The back door was unlocked. Mark opened it and called inside, his voice choked with misery.

"Mr. Shubert! He's gone! Are you up?"

"Come in, Mark. I'm in here!" The voice came from the living room. As he thought of Scruffy, out in the wind and rain, with no home or food, he was almost sick. He raced to the living room, closely followed by Dan.

In the doorway, Mark came to such a sudden halt that Dan bumped into him.

There on the couch, sitting next to Mr. Shubert, was Scruffy.

Mr. Shubert was eating oatmeal, and there was an empty, well-licked dish beside Scruffy.

The old man beamed at Mark. "He's come back," he chortled. "My little Scamp's come back! I said he would!"

Dan turned his bewildered eyes to look at Mark. "I thought you told me he was named Scruffy," he said, completely confused.

"It's not Scamp, Mr. Shubert!" Mark said in a loud voice, for the old man was almost deaf. "It's Scruffy. Remember? You let me keep him in your shed."

"I always said he'd come back!" Mr. Shubert repeated, his eyes shining, as he put an arm around Scruffy.

"You remember my little Scamp. He went away, and I said he'd come back."

"But, Mr. Shubert…" Mark began, and then he stopped. He took a few steps forward and sat down beside the little brown dog.

"Hello, little Scruff," he murmured, stroking the shabby fur. The dog wagged his tail and licked Mark's hand. "You remember me, don't you?" he said.

Then, sadly, he whispered, "It's no use. You just pretend to be Scamp, and I'll come over every day to visit and make sure that you have everything you need."

More puzzled than ever, Dan sat down next to Mark. "I thought he was named Scruffy," he repeated.

"He is."

"No he's not – he's named Scamp."

"I know."

Dan sighed. "I knew I shouldn't have gotten up so early," he said.

CHAPTER 5

Sharing

Mark and Dan walked slowly back from Mr. Shubert's house.

"You named him Scruffy," Dan said stubbornly. "Why did Mr. Shubert call him Scamp? Why aren't we bringing him back with us, like you said?" Poor Dan was mystified.

"About a year ago," Mark explained, "before you moved here, Mr. Shubert had a dog named Scamp. Then Scamp was run over by a car.

"Mr. Shubert just couldn't bear the idea that he didn't have his little dog anymore. I think he *wants* to believe Scruffy is really Scamp. They kind of look alike, I guess, especially because Mr. Shubert's eyes aren't so good."

"Scruffy was going to be yours." Dan looked puzzled. "Why didn't you tell Mr. Shubert that it wasn't Scamp? Then you could have brought Scruffy home."

Mark kicked at a stone. "I did," he replied slowly, "but Mr. Shubert didn't hear me, and he looked so happy."

Mark thought about Mr. Shubert's delighted face. Scruffy had looked pretty happy too.

Then he explained how he intended to go see Scruffy and take him for walks. Scruffy would still be his, really. He would even take dog food to Mr. Shubert. It would almost be the same.

Then Mark remembered Dad's job and the happiness at home. That had been because of Scruffy.

Putting on a brave face, he turned toward Dan.

"Anyway," he said, trying to sound cheerful, "I did have a dog for a day, didn't I?"

About the Author

This story began to
evolve in my mind
when I saw a little
brown dog tied to a
post, outside a store.

The dog was still there
when I came out of the store. He looked
so sad, sitting there all hunched and
trembling, his worried eyes watching.

The owner did come out of the store,
eventually, and was greeted by the little
dog, who was overjoyed! I began to
think about how important we are to
our dogs. They rely on us – and
sometimes their trust is betrayed. From
there, Scruffy and his story began.

Wendy Douthwaite